Contents

Rainforest life

Rainforests are places where rain falls in nearly every month, and where it is warm enough for trees to grow. Many parts of the world fit that description.

Most people, however, use the word rainforest to mean tropical rainforest, parts of the world close to the Equator where it is always humid and hot, and the temperature hardly varies throughout the year.

In these special places, as many species of wildlife live out their lives as in the rest of the world put together.

They are places of amazing adaptation and fierce competition, but even so, most wildlife finds it hard to compete with the pressure that people now put on their homes.

Fortunately what more and more people are coming to appreciate is that the rainforests, just like everywhere else on Earth, are the homes of other living things that need respect, too. To understand that better, turn the page.

▼ Parrots in the trees.

▼ Carrying logs out of a rainforest.

Where are the rainforests?

The weather near the Equator is nearly the same, some might say monotonously the same, all year round. There are no seasons such as winter and summer. It is also hot every day, and it rains most of the days in most of the months. This is why plants can grow all year.

Each day, however, has its own weather pattern. Day breaks sunny and clear, but clouds soon bubble up and, by afternoon, there is torrential rain. The rain stops about sunset, leaving a fine night with clear skies.

Although rain occurs on most days of most months, the world's largest rainforest, the Amazon, actually has a drier season, and this is when the forest grows the most. If you wanted to see the rainforest in sunlight, as opposed to it being dull and cloudy every day, you would choose June, July and August.

During the drier season, and without the clouds, the rainforest gets more sunlight, and as plants need sunlight to make their tissues (the process we call photosynthesis) this is when they grow the most.

The Amazon is so big that the rainforest year is different from place to place. To the north of the Equator, the rainy season is in June, July and August, but the majority of

▼ The world's tropical rainforests are close to the Equator. Here you can see the main ones. The UK is far away from the rainforests in a much cooler part of the world. (Source: Wikipedia)

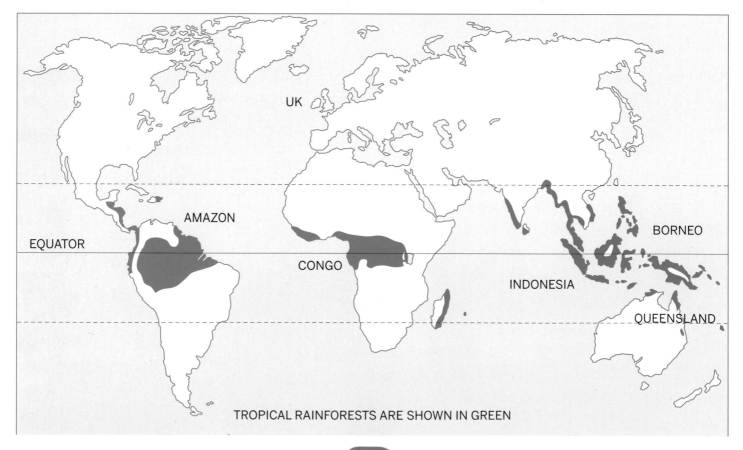

TROPICAL RAINFORESTS ARE SHOWN IN GREEN

the Amazon is south of the Equator, and over these areas, the rainy season starts somewhere around October or November, and ends somewhere between March and April, sometimes May.

Can you have tropical mountain rainforests?

If you go up a mountain it gets colder and the forest changes completely. This is why there are no tropical rainforests on the Andes, even though part of it is at the Equator.

On higher lands there are fewer plants and they grow more slowly. Curious though they are, they do not make rainforests, as you can see here. Tropical rainforests belong mainly to lowlands – places like the Amazon and Congo basins, Northern Australia and South Asia.

▲ Mountain rainforests are often shrouded in cloud and so are colder. Forests have less variety and grow more slowly.

▼ High mountains, such as Mt. Kenya, may be on the Equator, but the plants that grow are giant lobelias. It is too cold for trees. The photo was taken at about 4,000 m above sea level.

Deep, deep within the forest

This is the story about a part of the world where so many things live it is impossible to count them, or even to know how many species there are. Somehow they all survive. This is how.

It's a very strange thing, but when you see films of the tropical rainforest, you rarely see the forest. Instead you see monkeys and jaguars and ants and snakes. They are usually treated as though they moved about in some silent cathedral of pillars and beams.

People are fascinated by animals because they move, but the things they move among are alive, too. The 'pillars' are trunks of trees so varied that you might come upon more species in a five minute walk in a rainforest than you would if you walked the length and breadth of Britain.

The 'beams' are branches of trees that close together so precisely that they cut out all but about two per cent of the sunlight. The ropes that animals use to swing about on are alive, too. They are the stems of vines so long they could cover the side of a skyscraper.

Look closer

To see the trees and their differences, you have to look closely, and the closer you look, the more amazing they turn out to be.

Let's look at the riverside picture on page 8. It is full of sunlight, and there are plants at low level, at mid level and at high level. It's the sort of picture you often see of a rainforest because at a riverside you can stand far enough back to get a good shot. It tells us a lot, but to see just exactly what it tells us, we have to look inside the forest, away from the river. That is what you see in the picture above.

Same forest, same trees, but somehow it is completely different. Now you are inside the forest, you see mostly spindly trunks surrounding a few that are much larger. You see a few shafts of sunlight, but otherwise everything is dark and almost in silhouette. So where are all the lush green leaves of the picture opposite? The answer is that they are above you, high above you.

The secrets of growing

Tropical rainforests have, on average, the tallest trees in the world.

Think about a forest you might know close to home. Now double the height of the trees and that is what a typical tropical rainforest tree is like.

How a tree grows

The job of a tree – wherever it is – is to grow, set seed and produce new trees.

A tree grows by using its leaves to soak up energy. It also takes in carbon dioxide from the air and water, and minerals from the soil (or from decaying leaves, as we shall see later on).

Inside all green tissues there are tiny 'photocells' that soak up energy and use it in a way that can combine air, water and minerals to make leaves, stems, roots, petals and so on.

The photocells are called chlorophyll. The whole process is called photosynthesis and all life on Earth, including us, depends on it. That is because we eat plants, or we eat animals that have eaten plants.

By the way, roots (except aerial roots, page 34) stay white. This is because they don't have chlorophyll in them as they are never in the sunlight.

The stages of growing up

So how does a tree begin, and what are the stages that take it to be a big tree and part of the rainforest?

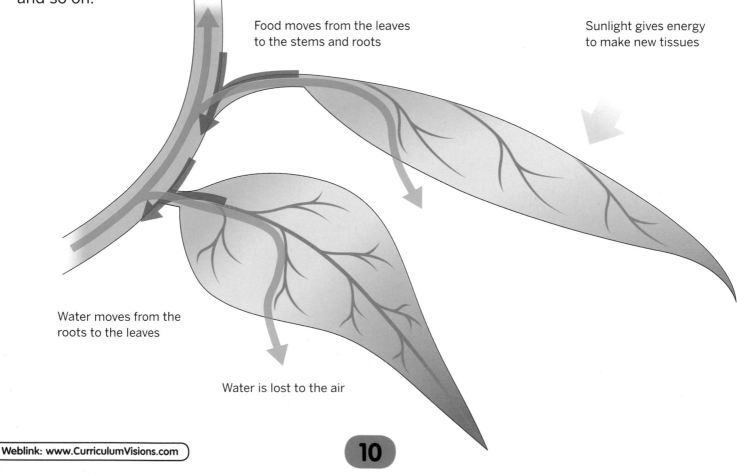

Food moves from the leaves to the stems and roots

Sunlight gives energy to make new tissues

Water moves from the roots to the leaves

Water is lost to the air

Making seeds, moving seeds

Plants begin as seeds.

Seeds are formed when pollen from one plant reaches another. Pollen is tiny. If there were strong winds, pollen would blow about with the wind and move between plants that way. But it is mainly calm in a tropical rainforest, so that method won't be very successful for rainforest plants.

The alternative is for a plant to encourage an animal to do the job of the wind. But insects are not interested in pollen. So they have to be attracted by devious means – a suitable smell and a suitable reward.

Just to make sure the insect gets to where the pollen is held, many plants also produce sugary nectar and have large, brightly-coloured flowers.

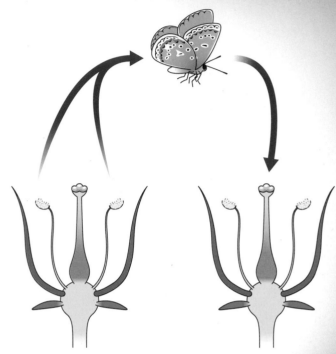

▲ Insects, including butterflies, and some small birds, like hummingbirds, are pollinators. The pollen is gathered from the little pads around the edge of the flower and rubbed off against the central stem of another flower.

▶ Hummingbirds, like insects, search inside flowers for nectar, and accidentally collect pollen. When they move to a flower on another tree, this pollen rubs off and fertilises the flower. Then seeds begin to form.

The world's biggest pong

There are as many species of plants in a tropical rainforest as in the rest of the world put together. They include the tiny and the huge. This is a picture of *Rafflesia arnoldii*, the world's largest flower. It is over a metre across and weighs 10 kilos. It is so heavy it has to rest on the forest floor. The flower lasts for just a few hours and smells like rotting meat – just the smell needed to attract the bugs it uses to carry its pollen.

Most of the flowers are produced just below the top of tree level, and this is, quite naturally, where most of the flying insects are, too.

Once a seed has been formed, it has to be put in a place where it stands the best chance of growing. That is, it has to be given a space of its own, some water to grow and preferably a supply of fertiliser to give it a good start. In many parts of the world, the wind carries seeds far and wide, sending out tens, or even hundreds of thousands of tiny seeds. But that is not much use in the rainforest. So the way plants move their seeds to different places is also different.

▼ This is a fruit from a tree called a Mameey apple, commonly known as a South American apricot. It has flowers and a shape like a magnolia, that is it has a short, stocky trunk and very long branches carrying hundreds of large flowers. Its leaves are leathery and grow to over 20 cm long. The tree grows to over 20 m tall and contains a natural insecticide to help protect it from plant-eating insects.

▲ Cupuaçu fruits belonging to a tree similar to a coco tree (cacao). The tree grows over 20 m tall and the fruits are 20 cm long and weigh up to 2 kg.

Cupuaçu fruit is one of the supposed health-giving 'superfruits' and you can find extracts of it in food supplements including pills, drinks, smoothies and sweets. It is a very good example of how much of a treasure-store the rainforest is.

▲ This is the seed pod of the Panama tree Apeiba aspera with germinating seedling. The seed is about 6 cm across.

Most plants produce a small number of seeds, but these are carefully wrapped up in a juicy fruit. The juice is not for the seed. The seed is the hard core to the fruit. The juicy fruit is to attract animals to eat it, and at the same time eat the seed.

The seed is often too tough to be broken down during digestion, so it travels right through the animal and is expelled in amongst its dung.

By now the animal has probably moved far from where it ate the fruit, so the plant has achieved what it set out to do: it has moved its seed to a new spot, and given it a bed of fertiliser to grow in. Now, over some days or weeks, the seed will start to grow, a process called germination.

Roots, shoots and leaves

A seed is a tiny plant with a small powerpack of food attached. The powerpack will not last long.

Roots first

When a seed germinates, the first thing it does is to send down a root and unfurl a pair of tiny leaves. It does not send up lots of leaves, it sends down a root. So what is so important about the root? The root does two things: it anchors the plant in the ground, and it gives it a way of collecting vital water and nourishment.

When it rains the leaves get wet, but the rain soon drips off. They are not a good way of collecting water. But when the rain drips into the ground, the tiny spaces between soil particles hold on to some of the water, just like the little holes in a sponge. That is a good way of storing water. So roots send out tiny root hairs which can dip in to each

of these tiny stores of water and help feed it back to the growing tree.

The root hairs also collect nourishment. Most nourishment comes from the rotting of old, dead trees. In the tropics, it rains so much that any nourishment released is quickly washed away. So how does a plant root get hold of this? The answer is by joining forces with tiny, almost microscopic living threads called fungi. Mushrooms are a fungus, but the fungus in a soil is simply long white threads. The fungus connects the rotting plants to the growing tree roots and passes food from one to the other (see page 28). Without the fungi, the trees would not grow well (and this is true throughout the world).

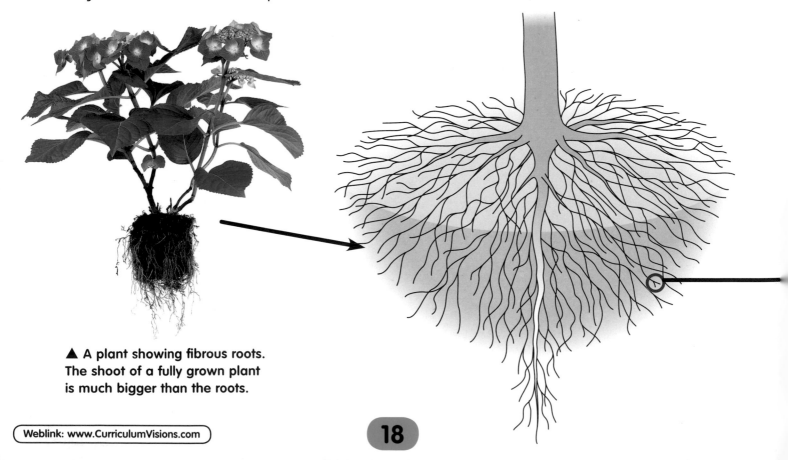

▲ A plant showing fibrous roots. The shoot of a fully grown plant is much bigger than the roots.

Then the shoot

The shoot is the part of the seedling that rises up from the seed. In a tree, this grows into the trunk and branches.

To begin with, plants use the nourishment in the seed, but that is soon used up, so they quickly have to fend for themselves. Now you see why 'root first' is so important.

Plant tissues are made of water, nourishment from the ground and carbon (dioxide) from the air, using sunlight as a source of energy. Given enough sunlight, warmth, moisture and nourishment the plants can now grow. Climbing plants have shoots that can become over a hundred metres long. They are mostly vines and their hanging stems are called lianes.

▼ The roots you can see have more tiny roots coming from them. They are called root hairs, and they collect water from the soil.

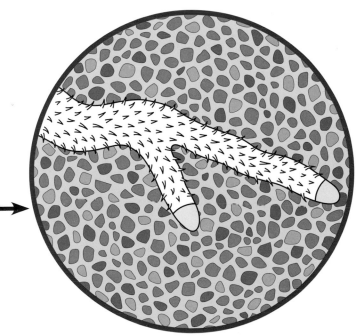

▲ The 'Swiss cheese plant', common in homes, is a climber from the tropical rainforest.

See a rainforest seed sprout

Below is a seed of a tree in the Amazon rainforest. It looks remarkably like a tree seed anywhere else in the world. Inside the seed are the parts that will grow, surrounded by a food supply.

If you follow the pictures below from left to right, you will see what happens. You may wish to compare it with other 'bean'-sized seeds, or grow a bean-sized seed for yourself.

There is a place on one end of the seed where growth begins. In this picture it is at the right-hand end.

Two things are happening more or less at the same time: a white shoot is unfolding out of the seed. It is almost like unfolding an umbrella. A pair of leaves are neatly folded in a compact shape, although they are, at this stage, tiny.

Below this shoot, and attached to it, you will notice, are the long white, stringy strands – the roots. There is a central, stocky root, and lots of smaller rootlets coming from it. It's like a river with tributaries, and indeed, the roots do the same kind of job, for they bring water into the main root and feed it up to the shoot, so the leaves and stem can swell and grow.

What you will also see is that the little leaves are white, but in the pictures on the right, they are red, then green. You will also see that the shoot rises and the leaves unfurl and grow. But without the root first firmly anchored into the soil, the tall shoot would simply fall over. Without the root, the shoot would not have a water supply to stay alive.

The powerpack of food in the seed is quickly used up, and the job of the leaves is to take over and soak up sunlight energy.

So here you can see a plant growing, as we imagine it might, in a soil in the Amazon rainforest. It is still tiny, so how will it turn into a huge tree?

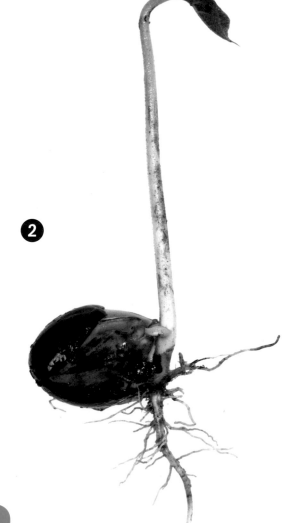

Evergreen, ever growing

A rainforest is a place where it is hot all of the time, and where it rains most of the time. So plants do not have different seasons as we have, or as you find in the savanna. As a result, the plants don't need to protect themselves from frost or drought by shedding leaves and 'hibernating'. That is why the plants in a rainforest can be broad-leaved evergreens.

Evergreens do not shed leaves in winter or in a dry season like deciduous plants. However, because a plant is evergreen it does NOT mean that it grows only one set of leaves and keeps them forever. On the contrary, an evergreen is always growing new leaves and shedding older ones.

If you study the rainforest you will find different trees budding or putting on leaves at different times of the year. They are more like leaf-exchanging trees. Unlike deciduous trees, they don't shed ALL their leaves over a short time because it gets cold or dry. Instead, they drop a leaf, perhaps because it has become old, and then put on a new leaf to replace it a few days later. Depending on the type of tree, a leaf can live anywhere from 12 months to nearly 4 years, but it does not live forever.

The fact that trees shed leaves is very important, because leaves contain nourishment for forest-floor animals and, when they decay, they release nourishment back to the soil so the trees can use it again.

Competing for space

The seeds we have just been looking at are not the only seeds about. There will be thousands more nearby. So each must struggle with its neighbours to win the precious place in the sun that will give it the energy to grow big and tall.

Now, when lots of plants grow close together, many only sense the light above them, so that is the direction they grow. There is no point having low branches with leaves on, for they will not get much light. Instead, they splay out branches only when they have got as far up as they can reach. It makes for a tall tree and a tall, straight trunk. In fact, in some ways, the trunk and branches look like a natural umbrella.

In the tropics, the Sun is overhead each day, so by spreading out crowns of branches that face upwards, trees get enough energy from sunlight for them to become giants.

On this page you see the conditions seeds begin in, and the change that happens when a tree falls, opening up a patch of forest floor to sunlight. You also see the race to grow.

▼ Seeds grow on a forest floor that is already the home to large trees which shade out the ground.

▲ From time to time, the large trees
die because they have become old.
This opens up a space in the rainforest.
The seedlings in that space grow greedily
towards the light. You can see them all
at the bottom of the picture above.

▼ Seedlings growing up in a clearing in
a race for the light. Because they are all
growing so close together, they are very
spindly at this stage.

This is a jungle

Compare it to the picture on the previous page. People have cut down some trees and let the light flood on to the forest floor. As a result all kinds of shrubs and trees are now growing fast as they make the most of the chance to capture sunlight. Eventually a few trees will grow up and shade out the ground. Many of the other plants will then die back, and the jungle will turn back into a rainforest. But it takes decades.

Rainforest roots

Some rainforest trees have roots that leave the main trunk above the ground. They are called buttress roots because some people think they hold up, or buttress, the main trunk.

What is common to all trees, even those without buttress roots, is that they spread out their roots just below the surface. They are not deep rooted.

When you see rainforest trees, you may think that such amazing trees must be growing out of deep, rich soil. But the soil is very poor. That is why the roots don't go down. Their nourishment comes from the decay of leaves that have died and fallen from the trees. So they spread out their roots like giant nets to capture all the nourishment back again. They also get amazing help from tiny white threads in the soil that are so small you can hardly see them. These white threads are called fungi. They rot the dead leaves, but grow on the live roots, so they transfer nourishment from leaf to root. It is incredibly efficient.

For most of the time, the fungi that help rot dead leaves and transfer the nourishment to tree roots are out of sight underground. But they have to produce their own 'seeds' (spores) and so, from time to time, they send up 'flowers' (fruiting bodies) which we call mushrooms and toadstools. Many are brightly coloured.

Forests of layers

A rainforest is not a collection of trees all at the same height. Rather, there are a number of layers.

Emergent trees

A few kinds of trees grow much taller and stick out from the gallery. No one knows why these 'emergent' trees do that, but it does give them more light.

The canopy trees

As it happens, many of the bigger tropical rainforest trees are much the same height. The forests are called gallery forests because all the branches are 'up in the gallery', like the highest seats in a theatre.

Understorey trees

Then, far below the canopy there are smaller trees, known as understorey trees. Many kinds of understorey trees would never grow tall even if you gave them lots of light. They have adapted to grow even with little light. Among them, however, are seedlings of the big trees that can't get enough light to grow up – for the moment.

The true understorey trees and shrubs tend to have big leaves, for big leaves soak up more light than small ones. Understorey trees with small leaves tend to be saplings waiting to grow into big trees.

So, if you look closely, you will find that a tropical rainforest can be divided into three layers – emergents, canopy and understorey, and that is what you can see in the diagram.

There is one more layer, and that is the plants that grow on the ground, but the ground in a rainforest is often quite bare and plants we might be used to, such as grass, do not grow on the floor of a rainforest. In fact, because of this, it is actually quite easy to walk around.

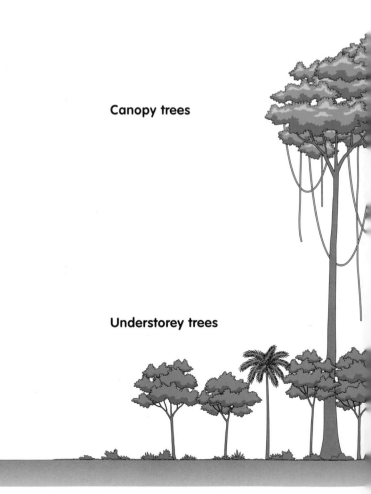

Emergent trees

Canopy trees

Understorey trees

Jungle

The forests that are hard to get through – and which most people call jungles – are those that have been altered by people. It is better always to use the term 'rainforest' when talking about forests that are still natural.

The word jungle should be used to talk about forests that have been severely disturbed by people. In fact, the word jungle comes from the Persian word meaning 'a tangled mass of plants that grow up when a cleared area has been abandoned'.

▼ This is a diagram that tries to show the three layers in a rainforest. To see what it actually looks like, see pages 32–33.

Lianes

▼ A tropical rainforest, showing the layers mentioned on the diagram on the previous page. The tourist observation hut gives an idea of scale.

Survival

How do plants survive in the rainforest? It is, to some extent, rather like the animals: they adapt to use a part of the forest that no other plant is using.

To see how this works, let's look at a variety of examples. Nearly all of these can be found in garden centres. Why? Partly because they are attractive, and partly because they are amazing survivors, managing to cope even when taken from their natural environment. Remember, however, that there are hundreds of thousands more species that we are not going to have the space to talk about.

The fig

Figs are very common rainforest trees. If you were to take a fully grown fig out of the rainforest you would find a cylinder of roots rising high into the air, and stems rising from this.

Most trees cannot grow much in the darkness of the forest floor, but figs are huge, so how do they get over this problem? Like most rainforest plants, they depend on animals to help. Birds and monkeys like the fig fruit and so they readily eat it, but the seed is not digested at all. As a result, the fig seed passes

right through the animal and comes out coated in nutritious dung.

Some seeds get dropped on the forest floor and probably never grow. But a lucky few seeds are deposited in the forks of branches high up in the trees. These seeds now begin to mature, sending down roots and sending up stems.

A fig can send roots down for tens of metres until they eventually find the soil. It also sends up stems that wrap themselves around the trunk of their host tree as they search for the light. A great tangle of roots and stems finally surrounds the tree where the seed first grew. They cover it so completely, the tree dies, but by this time the fig is able to stand upright on its own, with a ring of roots surrounding a decayed tree core. So, by using an adult tree as its host, the fig avoids competition for light and nutrients with other plants at ground level.

Bromeliads

Bromeliads, which are members of the pineapple family, have fans of leaves with tall coloured spikes, called bracts, rising from their centre. Like figs, they begin life high up in the forks of trees. But they do not send down roots and instead remain living in the trees throughout their lives. But without roots, how does the bromeliad live?

Bromeliads have thick, waxy leaves that overlap and tilt in towards the centre of the plant. Any rain that falls runs over the leaves, and in many cases forms a kind of tiny pond right in the centre of the plant. The biggest bromeliads make ponds that hold several litres of water. These ponds are home to other creatures, such as tree frogs and tadpoles, and even mosquito larvae.

Each of these creatures lives and dies in the bromeliad pond, and when it does its body decomposes and puts nourishment in the pond water, which the plant then extracts. Other creatures also fall into the pond and die, adding yet more nourishment.

▼ A bromeliad growing among the tangled vines and roots that are wrapped around this tree trunk. Below left (inset) bromeliads on trees in a dense rainforest (Queensland).

Orchids

Rainforest orchids, like bromeliads, live on a host tree. There are over 20,000 known species and most live in the tropical rainforests.

▼▶ Orchids live among the tree branches. They send out stiff stems completely covered with rows of beautiful flowers.

37

Pitcher plants

Some plants get their nourishment from animals in a more determined way. Pitcher plants have deep jug-like bowls. Many insects slip down the sides of the pitcher plant and drown in the water. The biggest of these is a vine called *Nepenthes rafflesiana*, which is found in the rainforests of South East Asia. It can climb tens of metres up a host tree. Its slender, green pitchers may be 30 cm long.

Lianes

These are vines, and often referred to as the ropes of the rainforest. Nine out of ten vines live in tropical rainforests. They have thick, woody stems that wrap themselves around the host tree, holding on fast with sucker roots, although they do not strangle their host like figs, for they need their host for support. They grow from the ground up into the tree canopy and then between trees. They can grow to enormous lengths and have been recorded as up to nearly a kilometre!

▼ **Look down into the bowls of these pitcher plants and see the dark water inside. It would be impossible for an insect to crawl out of the overhanging, slippery sides, so they simply drown. Then the liquids in the bowl dissolve them.**

▶ **Animals like sloths (shown here with a baby) and monkeys use lianes to move between trees without coming down from the canopy.**

Living together

This is the red-eyed tree frog, a native of Central American rainforests and a kind of emblem for rainforests.

This little chap is sitting on a leaf. He is watching for some food to come by.

The insects he eats may well have spent many months as caterpillars chomping away at rainforest leaves. So frog, insect, caterpillar and leaves are all connected. We call it a food chain.

Oh yes, and there is one more part of the food chain: the snake that is eyeing up the frog as a tasty morsel!

So, as he is not at the top of the food chain, this little chap needs his eyes to look both for food and for danger. Now you know why his eyes swivel on the top of his head!

▼ A red-eyed tree frog is much smaller than the main picture. It is just 2–4 cm long. This is its real size! Like many tree frogs, the red-eyed tree frog has suction cups on its toes that allow it to climb trees.

Plants get their nourishment from the ground. All other living things get their nourishment by eating plants or other animals.

Animals that eat plants are called herbivores. Animals that eat other live animals are called carnivores. Animals that eat dead animals are called scavengers, if they are large. Tiny animals (wood lice, termites, fungi, bacteria and so on) that eat dead material and release nourishment for plants to use again are called decomposers. All these types of animals make a cycle of life.

The rule of life

Food gives the body energy to keep on working. So when animals eat food they are, in a way, eating energy. However, when one thing eats another, not all the energy is passed on because most of it is used up in living.

There is a simple rule of living wherever you are in the world. Every time something eats something else, it can only get about a tenth of the energy. The energy starts out in sunlight. Plants capture that and make tissue. But when a caterpillar, for example, eats a plant leaf, it cannot get all of the sun's

Parts of a rainforest food chain

1 Most animals eat plants, but each species will only eat certain kinds of plant; any one species cannot eat all plants.

The Okapi is a plant-eating animal. It looks like a cross between a zebra and a horse, but it is actually related to the giraffe. Like the giraffe, the Okapi has a very long tongue that can reach out and pull tender new leaves off forest trees (it can even use its tongue to groom its ears!).The Okapi isn't nearly as tall as the giraffe. It stands only about 1.5 metres tall. It was only discovered in 1900. The Okapi lives mainly in rainforests in northern Zaire.

2 Most meat-eating animals (carnivores), such as jaguars, pumas and tigers, will eat a range of animals – more or less anything they can catch. This gives them more of an opportunity to find food. This Jaguar's spots help it to blend into the background, so it can ambush its unwary prey. Most of its prey see in black and white, not colour.

energy that was used in making the leaf. When a frog eats a caterpillar, it cannot get all of the energy that was used in keeping the caterpillar alive.

Because of this, most of the world has to be plants. The second most common living thing has to be plant-eating animals. The least common living thing has to be animal-eating animals.

Here is another result: a plant can grow on a small patch of land. An elephant has to roam through the forest eating lots of branches from many trees, So its 'territory' is larger. A tiger has to go wandering about looking for other animals to eat. If it stayed in one place and simply waited for its food to walk by, it would starve.

So now you know why you see lots of insects, quite a few frogs and not many snakes, for example.

Food chain

What we have been looking at are examples of what scientists call a food chain. It is incredibly important, for it tells us how the rainforest works and, in the long run, tells us how to look after the environment. It's so important, it is worth going over again.

Without any plants all animals would die.

3 Vultures are scavengers. They eat dead carcasses. But they are just as vital a part of the cycle of life as all other creatures. When the meat has been stripped off the carcass, insects, and finally bacteria, will finish it off. So many animals get nourishment to keep living. This is a black vulture of South America which prefers open land by rivers.

So if you cut down the rainforest, animals that live in it cannot survive.

▶ If too many animals eat all the plants, they will have nothing left to eat and they will starve.

▶ If we cut down the rainforest trees and replace them with grass, most animals will still die (trees produce far more food than grass on the same space, and it is different food, too).

Here are some examples again:

If snakes eat too many frogs, there will not be enough frogs to breed, and there will not be enough frogs for the snakes, and many snakes will die. That gives frogs a chance to start breeding again.

Do you see how important all of this is? Do you see that everything is in a seesaw balance? It's not as though a tiger says to itself: that's enough wild boar for this year because I am worried about the food balance. The tiger just eats what it can all the time. Well-fed tigers result in large, healthy litters of cubs. But if too many tigers are born they will eat up too many wild boar and so, in a year or two, food will become scarce and some tigers will die. With fewer tigers about, the animals that are their food will start to become more common again. No animal thinks about this. It just happens, and sometimes it looks harsh and pitiful. But in the grand scheme, everything stays in balance.

The thing about a rainforest is that it has a huge amount of food in a wonderful variety. So a wonderful variety of animals make use of it. Some can use the plants in the canopy. Some use the fruits lower down, and some eat what falls to the ground. Now we can look at some of the animals that make use of each piece.

▲ This diagram shows some of the more well known, or more common, animals of a rainforest.

You may now realise that they all depend on one another because they are all parts of a food chain.

Harpy eagle

Vulture

Sloth

Morpho butterfly

Bird of paradise

Emerald tree boa

Howler monkey

Flying fox

Red-eyed tree frog

Large beetles living on the soil

Humming bird

Millipede

Ant

Green iguana

Small beetles and crustaceans
(like woodlice) living in the soil.

Although there are huge numbers of animals
in a rainforest, when you walk in a rainforest
you may see almost nothing but trees. The next
page shows you why.

Bugs

A large part of the life of many bugs is usually spent as something else, for example, a caterpillar or a grub.

Insects lay eggs by the billion, and caterpillars munch leaves by the billion, too. Some adult insects, such as many butterflies, do not eat at all, but simply live for a few days, lay eggs and die. Others live for many years.

Each plant-eater tends to specialise in one kind of food. That is how so many species can survive without taking away the food of others. Some eat live leaves, others eat dead leaves, some live in the tops of trees, some fly about in the canopy, while others crawl about the forest floor or live in the soil. Remember, there is more mass of bugs (insects, spiders, etc) than all other animals put together. You sometimes see them, especially if they are poisonous, you often hear them, but for most of the time most insects keep out of the way, or camouflage themselves because they know they will make a tasty morsel for birds,

▲ Most butterflies suck nectar from flowers.

▼ Recently-hatched caterpillars munching their way through a leaf.

▼ An insect camouflaged as a leaf.

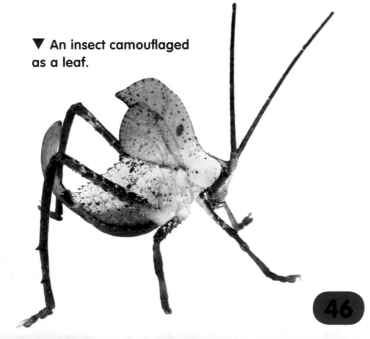

▲ Atlas Moths (which are found in
tropical Asia) are the largest moths
in the world and have a wingspan
of 25 cm.

▲ Giant Amazonian caterpillar on a tree trunk.

◄ Ground beetles are plant-eaters, with many specialising in eating dead leaves and wood.

▼ Millipedes are vegetarians, and in tropical rainforests can grow to nearly 30 cm.

▲ Beetles are among the most common of insects. Many of them eat fruit. Other fruit-eaters include wasps and bees.

▼ Dragonflies are hunters.

reptiles and small mammals. They will also make a good meal for other bugs.

The most numerous bugs include beetles (the most common of all insects), and varieties of ant, including termites. Ants and termites are mainly vegetarians, although ants will certainly overpower and eat any other insect that comes within reach.

Ants have nests that form mounds on the rainforest floor. Termites almost never come to the surface, and have white bodies. When they go foraging to find more dead wood, they build tunnels for themselves out of scraps of plant and dung. Their nests are mainly below ground, but they build mud 'castles' partly above ground in order to help provide 'chimneys' to suck fresh air into their nests.

◄ Spiders are common in rainforests. Some make webs, many others lie in wait for their prey and then pounce. Tarantulas are pouncing spiders. They can spin silk, but they do not use this to make a web, rather, to make a kind of tented tube home.

▲ Termites at work in their burrows.
Termites mainly eat dead wood.

▼ Ants foraging for food on
a leaf. Ants will eat many
kinds of food, including the
bird dropping on this leaf.

Reptiles

Rainforests have a huge variety of reptiles, the biggest of which is the crocodile (or alligator in the Americas).

Small reptiles, such as frogs, eat insects. A large reptile will eat anything that comes within its reach. Reptiles can move very quickly over short distances, but do not have much stamina so cannot chase things. As a result, many reptiles are camouflaged, so they can lie in wait and ambush their prey as it comes within reach.

Reptiles are cold-blooded, egg-laying animals such as lizards, frogs, snakes and crocodiles. Being cold-blooded means they rely on the heat of the air or of sunshine to help them move. However, this has its advantages. Because they don't use most of their food energy in keeping warm (as we do), they can survive for very long periods without eating.

Most of them live on, or close to, the ground or in water. This is because many reptiles (and especially frogs) have skin that lets moisture and oxygen in. For this to work, they need to be in a moist place. If conditions are dry for too long, frogs risk losing too much water through their skins, and dying. A rainforest is an ideal place for a reptile because it is always warm and mostly moist.

Because they are common and mostly small, they are ideal food for many mammals, and even some large insects. The way they protect themselves is partly by being brightly coloured and poisonous, having colours similar to poisonous relatives, by camouflage and also by being able to dart away from danger quickly. Even a snake will slither away rather than attack a large animal.

▲ A camouflaged iguana.

► Most rainforest frogs are very small. Many are tree-dwellers and can climb lianes, as this one is doing.

▼ A small gecko lizard. Geckos make a characteristic chirping sound. They also have special pads on their toes which allow them to cling on to smooth surfaces such as leaves.

▼ A crocodile waiting to pounce.

Birds

Most birds eat insects or seeds. In a rainforest, the majority of flowers and fruits are high up near the top of the trees. Many insects fly about in and above the top of the trees (the canopy) in search of nectar and so this is where most birds are, too.

One in five of all the birds in the world lives in the rainforests of the Amazon, but although you may hear them, they are difficult to spot because they are high up in the canopy. And, although we may know of brightly coloured macaws and toucans, many birds are camouflaged and so are green or brown.

Of course, some birds live near the ground. For example, egrets (picture below) live close to rivers and lakes. Vultures eat dead carcasses, and these are always on the ground, so that is where vultures lurk, too.

▲ Toucans do not crush seeds as parrots do, but eat fruit and swallow the seeds. As a result, they are very useful in spreading tree seeds about.

▲ Parrots

▲ Many vultures soar over the rainforest looking for carcasses. But vultures will also eat nuts (such as coconuts) if carcasses are difficult to find.

Parrots

Parrots are common rainforest birds. They have a strong curved bill, strong legs, and are mostly green, with flashes of bright colour. Cockatoos have a crest of feathers on the top of their heads.

Parrots mainly eat seeds, nuts, fruit and buds. Parrots do not eat fruit except to get at the seed, so they are not useful to plants needing their seeds scattered.

The powerful bill makes opening the husks (seed cases) and eating seeds quite easy. The parrot turns the husk in its mouth, crushing more of the husk with each turn. Some seeds have poisonous coatings, but parrots strip off most of this coating and also eat clay to neutralise the poisons. Parrots nest in tree holes, and fly in the tree canopy because this is where most seeds are found.

Weblink: www.CurriculumVisions.com

◀ Wild boar are some of the largest plant-eaters. They dig their snouts into the soil seeking roots as well as eating fruit, nuts and berries that drop from the canopy. They will also eat small dead animals, insects and small reptiles.

▼ The Asian elephant can be recognised by its small ears.

Mammals

Mammals are warm-blooded animals that have fur or hair, and that give birth to, and suckle, live young.

Tropical rainforests are home to many kinds of mammals, ranging in size from tiny mice to forest elephants. The biggest mammals like elephants, cats (tigers, jaguars) and mammals related to us (including monkeys and apes) – called primates – are a familiar sight in zoos and on wildlife films. But most rainforest mammals are small, are active at night (they are nocturnal), and are not easily seen. For example, bats and rodents (rats, mice, and so on) are the most plentiful mammals in most rainforests.

Thinking about the way the food chain works helps us to understand this. Hunting animals are always less common than plant-eating animals. Small animals can usually find lots of little places to live. Large animals cannot. Small mammals only need small territories, large animals need huge territories. Most hunters are only active in the day.

Elephants

The larger plant-eaters are the animals best known to us.

The Asian elephant is a forest-dweller. Elephants move in small herds, eating ten per cent of their body weight each day – about 200 kilos of food. They are not very efficient at making use of the food they eat, which is why they leave huge piles of dung behind them. This dung is not wasted, but is food for a multitude of other small animals. Some sort through the dung to find food that has not been digested at all. Others need partly digested food as they can't eat living plants directly.

55

Monkeys, gorillas, lemurs…

Monkeys belong to a group of animals that include lemurs and apes. Most monkeys have tails; apes do not. The term 'monkey' is an artificial grouping, used much like we would use the word 'fish'.

The smallest monkeys are about 15 cm long, and the largest – the Mandrill – is about a metre. Most of them eat fruit, leaves, seeds, nuts, flowers, eggs, and they also eat insects and spiders. Many monkeys live high in the trees, but the Mandrill scavenges about the forest floor.

Big cats

Big cats are at the top of the food chain and as they directly compete with people, their numbers have fallen sharply, and they are now endangered species.

▲ Gorillas are the largest of the living apes. They live on the ground, eating mainly leaves, fruits and shoots. Because plant leaves contain less nourishment than nuts or meat, gorillas have to spend most of the day eating.

◄ The male Proboscis Monkey has a very large nose, which is attractive to the female monkeys. All Proboscis Monkeys have large bellies. This is because their diet of leaves releases a lot of gas.

▼ Golden Lion Tamarins like to live in canopy forests with many vines and bromeliads. The closed canopy and tangles of vines provide protection while the bromeliads host many insects, which are the Tamarins' main food.

◀ Lemurs are found only on Madagascar and nearby islands. Some lemurs are tiny and weigh little more than 30 g, while the largest weighs 10 kg. Lemurs eat fruit, flowers and leaves as well as insects, spiders and small animals.

▼ Orangutans are the largest tree-living animal and have longer arms than other apes. They are members of the great apes. Every night they make sleeping nests from branches and leaves. They are more solitary than other apes, and the mothers stay with their babies for several years. They mainly eat pulpy fruits such as figs, but they also eat young leaves, shoots, bark, insects, honey and bird eggs.

Orangutans are thought to be the sole means of scattering the seeds of some fruit trees. If the orangutan becomes extinct, so will the trees that depend on it.

Big cats and other large hunters are vital to the natural food chain. They stop numbers of other animals growing out of control.

Big cats have markings that help them blend in with their surroundings. It is not possible to chase an animal in a rainforest as it would be on savanna plains, so these big cats hunt patiently, moving silently through the forest until they get close enough to spring on their prey. They eat a huge variety of animals, from fish and crocodiles to wild pigs and deer.

The jaguar is the third-largest large cat after the tiger and the lion. It looks like a leopard, but behaves like a tiger. Both tigers and jaguars are good swimmers. Jaguar eat deer, capybara, tapirs, peccaries, sloths, monkeys and turtles – and their powerful bite means that they can even eat armadillos.

In general, the jaguar feeds on larger animals. The cougar is a slightly smaller animal, and feeds mainly on smaller animals, which is how the two can exist together.

▼ **Asian tiger.**

▶ **South American jaguar.**

Fruit bats

Most rainforest mammals are small and live high in the canopy or in burrows in the forest floor. Here you see fruit bats. Fruit bats are the largest type of bat. They are typical of animals that spread seeds. Bats spit the seeds out when they have eaten the surrounding fruit. Nectar-drinking fruit bats also pollinate plants.

So, what do we know now?

We have now come to the end of this book, although you should note the three related books – 'Exploring the endangered rainforest', 'Exploring rainforest people' and the Creative Topic virtual book 'Rainforest bugs'.

This book is designed to give you a broad understanding of how the natural rainforest works. 'Exploring the endangered rainforest' tells you a bit more about the effects of people, 'Rainforest bugs' tells you much more about the biggest number of species – bugs, and 'Rainforest people' tells you about the people who live in the rainforest, those who live with it, and those whose actions are destroying it.

In summary: the facts

Tropical rainforests lie in the 'tropics', within about 10 or 15 degrees of the Equator. They are not the hottest places in the world, but the temperatures are always in the 20s or 30s °C. There are no big seasonal swings in temperature. The difference between the warmest and coldest months may be as little as 0.3°C.

Tropical rainforests get over 2,000 mm of rainfall each year, spread fairly evenly throughout the year. It never dries out enough to force plants to shed their leaves, so rainforest plants are evergreens.

There is enough rain to allow broad-leafed evergreen trees to be the normal kind of rainforest tree.

An average canopy tree sucks up through its roots about 750 litres of water a day, and sends this out as water vapour through its leaves (it's called transpiration).

So much water vapour is released that rainforests help to make their own clouds, and this produces half of the rain that falls back on the forest.

Tropical rainforests cover less than two per cent of the Earth's surface, but they are home to half of all life on the

planet. (The ocean equivalent is the coral reefs, see the Creative Topic book 'Life and death on a coral reef').

No one knows how many different kinds of living thing there are in tropical rainforests, perhaps somewhere between 5 million and 50 million species. We don't know this number because we have not had time to look properly.

How do we get an idea of this variety? One of the best ways is by comparing trees. In a hectare of woodland in Britain there might be half a dozen different tree species. In a tropical rainforest of the same size, there might be nearly 500 different species of tree!

If we look at animals we see the same thing. The same hectare of land in a rainforest might be home to more species of ant than live in the whole of Britain.

The whole of the population of London could be fitted into a single nest (colony) if we were ants!

In 260 hectares (1 sq mile) of rainforest there might be more than 50,000 insect species.

170,000 of the world's 250,000 known plant species are found in rainforests.

A third of the world's bird species are found in the Amazon rainforest.

Over three quarters of the animals in a rainforest live in the canopy, high above the forest floor.

◀ Tiger

Index